Bring Yourself to the Table

Bring Yourself to the Table

A Path to Remembrance for
Every Mother, Wife, and Woman
Who has Abandoned Herself

Kelly Marsh

Bring Yourself to the Table
© 2025 Kelly Marsh
All rights reserved.

No part of this book may be reproduced, stored in a retrieval system, or transmitted in any form or by any means—electronic, mechanical, photocopying, recording, or otherwise—without prior written permission from the publisher, except for brief quotations in reviews or critical articles.

This book is a work of creative expression.
Names, characters, and events are drawn from the author's life and imagination. Any resemblance to actual persons, living or dead, is coincidental or used with permission.

Published by Marsh Unlimited, LLC
Interior and illustrations by Kelly Marsh
Cover design by Kelly Marsh
Printed in the United States of America

ISBN 979-8-9940314-0-7

First Edition 2025

A gift for my sons.

May this book help you understand the women you will one day love,
their tenderness, their strength,
their quiet battles and unseen burdens.

May it teach you to listen with your whole heart
and to honor their stories, even when they are hard to hear.

And when you love a woman,
may you become the kind of man who stands *with* her,
never above her and never against her,
and who never asks her to stand alone.

Author's Preface

This book began as a quiet rebellion.

For years I lived beneath the weight of what a woman was told she must be:
soft, small, agreeable, holy.
I mistook silence for peace and obedience for love.
But the longer I tried to be the model of a perfect girl and woman,
the farther I drifted from myself.

These poems trace the path toward myself,
not back to the girl I used to be,
but to the woman I was never allowed to become.
They follow the breaking open, the reckoning,
the small, brave moments when I chose my own voice
over the comfort of approval.

Healing, I've learned, is not a return. It is a
growth that seeks light even after years of shadow.
It's becoming who you are *because* of what you survived,
not in spite of it.

If you see yourself anywhere inside these pages,
I hope you feel not shame, but recognition.
I hope you see that the weight you carried was never proof of your weakness.
It was the measure of your strength.

This is a book for the women learning to stand without apology.
For the one who finally realizes she was never too much
the world simply asked her to be less.

These poems rise from pieces of my own life, but they also hold echoes of
the women I love and the stories we've shared.
Some poems come from my experience; others are shaped by the collective
weight women carry every day.
Many are written in a universal voice, a poetic "she," so that any woman might
see herself reflected in these pages.

TABLE OF CONTENTS

Prologue

The Weight of Her Sky

Part I — The Becoming

She Was Born of Light
Through Her Eyes
The Rules of the House
The Way I Was Raised
Promises He Never Meant
The Years I Straightened My Hair
High Desert Days
Eighteen

Part II — The Promise

The Promise
The Forest Wedding
Fear of a Good Kind
The Honeymoon
The Heart Outside My Body
The Joys of Motherhood

Part III — The Fracture

The Weight of Doing All
The Vampire
The Turning
Shrinking
The Colors I Erased
The Storm Within Walls
Just Sinking

Part IV — The Undoing

The Life That Stays Behind
Fault Line
Suspended
After the Burning
The Stranger in the House
The House That Words Undid
The Weary One
For My Sister
Vanishing
Grace
The Hidden Place Within Me
The Evidence
The Breaking Point
Just Today
The Leaving
The Empty House
Life Sentence

Part V — The Rising

She Keeps Rising
Clarity
Where Quiet Lives
The Bloom After
Caring Too Much
Becoming Whole
I Let My Curls Be Free
A World Without Masks
What I Keep
The Wholeness of Me

Part VI — The Table (The Return)

The Breath
The Measure of Love
And So I Stayed
For the Mother Who Hopes After Loss
Bring Yourself to the Table
The Cabin We Built
The Seat Beside Them

Epilogue

The Invitation
For the Woman Who Sat Quietly

Before You Continue

This book moves like life does—through shadow and softness, hurt and hope. Some poems may feel heavy; some may feel like relief.

If you need to set the book down, please do. If you want to skip ahead to Part V — The Rising for steadier ground before returning, honor that.

But if you're able, I encourage you to read the poems in order—because the journey matters. The darkness is not the destination. The arc bends toward healing, strength, and return.

So just hold on, because this path winds, falls, and—most importantly—rises.

Just like we do.

PROLOGUE

The Weight of Her Sky

She shoulders dawn, the weight, the span,
an Atlas bound by mortal hands.
The sky she lifts is endless, wild,
the world she holds, each dreaming child.

Like Sisyphus, she wakes to climb,
the same steep hill, the same old time.
Her back is bent, her breath is fire;
the stone betrays her, but she climbs higher.

Like Prometheus, her gift is flame;
she gives them wisdom, love, a name.
They feast unknowing on her core;
each day she breaks to give them more.

The eagle comes, her heart its prize,
and still she meets it steady-eyed.
The gods bear witness from above,
yet offer neither shield nor love.

They call her strong and praise her grace,
while tears carve furrows through her face.
And still she lifts, and still she gives,
her myth the very life she lives.

The gods look down but never see
the weight of sky, the ache of she.

PART I – THE BECOMING

She Was Born of Light

Before the world had learned to spin,
before the breath of life blew in,
a hush fell thick; the stars took flight,
and from that stillness came her light.

The sky was ink, the sea was sleep,
the mountains mused in silence, deep.
The wind reached out, the earth drew near,
and whispered, *Child, awaken here.*

From molten core and silver mist,
her brow the dawn itself had kissed.
Her tears grew roots; her joy sprawled wide,
and something ancient stirred inside.

She walked through nothing, shaping form,
a heart half wildfire, half newborn.
The sun knelt low to touch her face
and thus began the human race.

Through Her Eyes

The first thing I remember was her face,
soft, but dimmed around its grace.
Her eyes were red from nights awake.
Her smile felt forced, her hands would shake.

She whispered *hi*, her voice withdrawn,
then looked past me and she was gone.
I felt her reach then pull away,
a warmth too faint, afraid to stay.

Her love was there, but stretched too thin,
a trembling glass she lived within.
I sensed the ache she couldn't hide,
a hunger love could not provide.

Somewhere beyond the sterile air,
I knew she longed for someone there.
Not me, not yet, just someone's hand,
a promise she could not command.

The nurses smiled; the world was kind,
but she was left somewhere behind.
Her body near, her spirit gone,
I felt her loss before the dawn.

Still in her arms before the years,
before her hope was drowned by fears,
I breathed her sorrow, love, and fight,
and promised her I'd turn out right.

The Rules of the House

The air went quiet when he came home.
His boots made thunder down the stone.
We'd learned the signs, the creak, the door.
To freeze, to hush, to be no more.

He never yelled; he didn't need.
A look could make the body plead.
The paddle slept above the door,
its holes like eyes that promised more.

I learned to stand, to not ask why,
to count the seconds, not to cry.
The sun would sink, the day would fade.
I'd wait for night, but not be saved.

He built new rules, each one to prove
his strength, his right, his power's groove.
My mother moved, but wasn't there,
a ghost in skin, an empty stare.

He never loved. I knew the cost:
a house half-lived, a childhood lost.
And every night the house would sigh,
a warning not to meet his eye.

From him I learned what men would do,
that love could wound and still feel true.
I carried that into my years,
a language written first in fear.

The Way I Was Raised

I was raised to keep the peace,
to speak in tones that never crease,
to smooth the edge of every word,
so I'd be seen but barely heard.

I was taught that kindness means
to shrink my wants and guard my dreams,
to smile when things felt out of place,
to hide discomfort with my grace.

They praised my quiet, called it sweet,
while boys ran feral with untamed feet.
Their laughter loud, their tempers praised,
while mine was tamed and swiftly caged.

When teenage eyes began to roam,
I learned my body wasn't home,
to laugh off things that crossed the line,
and call it fine, to stay benign.

I felt their stare though they were grown,
a child in bodice not her own.
I hid the curve, the shape, the glow,
and prayed no gaze would let it show.

I heard the jokes, the tired kind,
where women shrink in every line.
I wore a smirk, ignored the tone,
till all my softness turned to stone.

They said *be nice*, not *speak your name*,
as if my pain deserved the blame.
To never yell, nor make a scene,
I learned to silence what I'd seen.

They ran through mud and broke the rules,
were called *just boys*, while girls stayed tools.
We learned to serve, to bow, to mend,
to lose ourselves, then love again.

We learned to read the room, the tone,
to soothe the woe we hadn't sown,
to patch the wounds that weren't our own,
to call that care, and call it *home*.

We hushed our cries so others slept,
and bore their hurt while ours was kept.
We tended embers, made cold hearts warm,
yet none reached out to calm our storm.

I was raised to not take up space,
to tame my hair, stay in my place.
And as I grew they said *be kind*,
as if that meant to lose my mind.

Now grown, I see the gentle guise,
how grace was built on sacrifice.
I shed the roles the world required,
and freed the self they once desired.

Promises He Never Meant

You said you'd be here, but never came,
a broken vow and shifted blame.
I waited long past what was fair,
a child guarding an empty chair.

I learned that hope can scorch and sting,
that promises mean not a thing.
And now when someone swears they're true
my heart steps back,
because of you.

The Years I Straightened My Hair

I learned to fight my hair each day,
to burn the wild, to smooth the sway.
The mirror whispered, *you'll fit in soon*,
the hiss of heat, a siren's tune.

The magazines all showed one face,
a thinner girl, a softer grace.
I brushed until my scalp would sting,
and cursed the crown my roots would bring.

Each tug a tear, each tear a plea,
to be the girl they'd want to see.
My frizz, defiant, caught their stares,
as though my worth was less than theirs.

They declared it polished, called it neat,
to crush the curls beneath my feet.
And every strand I forced to lie
became the truth I learned to buy.

Now even rain feels like a test.
I flinch when weather leaves a mess.
The girl inside still smooths her pain,
and irons truth to look the same.

High Desert Days

We smelled the sage through sun and dust.
Our tires hissed, as goatheads thrust.
We patched them laughing, side by side,
then raced again before they dried.

The river roared beneath the bridge.
We leapt from rails and canyon ridge.
At Lucky Peak, the mountain lake,
its icy breath made bodies quake.

When snow turned sharp and ice grew long,
we sought the springs where warmth was strong.
The air was thick with sulfur steam,
the stars above a river's gleam.

We pulled the e-brake just to spin.
Snow haloed headlights, joy and wind.
The night was ours, the valley wide,
the stars our map, the dark our guide.

None of us knew what we'd lose,
how quickly youth outgrows its shoes.
We didn't know the world would bend,
that summers fade and moments end.

Eighteen

The world was ripe, the air was sweet,
a steady beating in my feet.
I'd never heard, but somehow knew,
a rhythm thrumming what to do.

I caught my shape in passing glass,
the curve, the sway, the girl now cast.
No longer hiding, unmarked by shame,
I traced my lips and spoke my name.

I imagined hands both kind and new,
of what they'd seek, of what they'd do,
of love that sparked, of words that stay,
of nights that taught and dawns that fray.

My body stirred, alive, aware,
a secret warmth electric there.
The future gleamed so vast, so near,
I met it without doubt or fear.

And somewhere in that tender start,
I pined for hands to hold my heart.
Not conquest, nor claim, nor fleeting play,
but someone who would choose to stay.

PART II – THE PROMISE

The Promise

I didn't know what vows could weigh.
I only knew his eyes that day.
The world was gold, the air was kind,
and every doubt was left behind.

We dreamed that we could stitch the sky,
that love alone could never die.
The path was set, my heart was sure,
I thought forever would endure.

The Forest Wedding

The morning woke in hush and green,
where light through trembling branches leaned.
A bouquet of flowers, woven thread,
daisies circled round her head.

A dress stitched slow by patient hands,
with lace that promised wedding bands.
The wind had paused, the robins stayed,
as if the world itself delayed.

She walked the path through birch and fern,
the soft earth cool, the daylight turned.
Each step a vow the forest kept,
while golden motes around her swept.

He turned his eyes a steady tide,
where every doubt and wish could hide.
Their hearts unscarred began to weave,
the myths they'd one day both believe.

For love was young and hope was wild,
the dream still virgin, undefiled.
The forest bore its witness true,
to love that opened brave and new.

Fear of a Good Kind

The air was brushed by something new,
a tender shift I barely knew.
My breath turned light, my pulse unstrung,
a trembling hush of being young.

His closeness moved the room to still,
an offering shaped by patient skill.
No force, no rush, no hurried part,
just steady warmth and subtle art.

His fingertips moved, not to claim,
but asked permission all the same.
A courage formed where fear had stayed,
a hidden stirring long delayed.

It flickered once, then fell away;
I let a braver trust make way.
And in that space where shadows part,
I felt the opening of heart to heart.

The Honeymoon

We skimmed the edge of foreign skies,
our laughter stitched through long goodbyes.
The world was vast, yet somehow small,
when hand in hand we had it all.

The roads were dust, the nights were wide,
a single suitcase by our side.
We danced through rain and borrowed towns
and slept beneath the thunder's sound.

We learned the taste of sweet and strange,
our hearts unhurt, unbruised by change.
The future was an open shore,
and every road led back to more.

Your fingers traced the map we'd made,
the ink still wet, our plans unlaid.
We didn't need to know what's true,
the world felt right because of you.

The Heart Outside My Body

The air was thick with rising heat,
the drum of life beneath my feet.
The earth leaned close, the sky grew small,
and I became the pulse of all.

Each wave that came, I met its crest,
a creature fierce, unshod, undressed.
The room dissolved, the hours blurred.
The primal song was all I heard.

My bones remembered what to do,
a rhythm older than I knew.
Through pain and power, blood and grace,
the universe passed through this space.

A cry rose up, the world stood still,
and every ache was mercy's will.
Your nearness met my shaking spine,
the breaking drew a sacred line.

You lay upon me damp and new,
your heartbeat echoed mine in two.
My heart, once guarded deep inside
now lives where I can't let it hide.

I cradle you, the world transformed,
both fierce and fragile, newly formed.
And in this world, I understand:
creation rests in human hands.

The Joys of Motherhood

There were days you couldn't stand to be
a single step away from me,
bending low to meet the floor,
slipping fingers beneath the door.

You'd taste the world in hurried bites,
eyes wide with laughter, pure delight.
Each meal a feast, each mess a song.
I blinked and those small years were gone.

You'd sing yourself to sleep at night,
your lullabies a fragile light.
I'd sit outside and softly cry,
in awe of how the days go by.

You ran through halls in droll parade,
a diaper crown your grand crusade.
Your naked joy, your fearless art,
it carved a smile upon my heart.

Your first small goal, your name, the cheer,
I swear the whole world stopped to hear.
Your tiny cleats at rest upstairs,
the proof that love still lingers there.

You learned to swim without your wings,
the water held you, you daring thing.
You kicked, you gasped, the sunlight played,
and pride blazed bright in all we made.

You learned to ride, to fall, to spin,
to scrape your knees, then start again.
A tricycle's rush, a wheelie's thrill,
the wind would bow beneath your will.

Behind the couch you'd hide your trash,
the secret hoard of snacks you'd stashed.
Your chocolate hands, your guilty grin,
I laughed, then let you hide again.

Each look, Mom, look, a holy plea,
a call for eyes to truly see.
You taught me joy in loud small ways,
to see the world through your amaze.

We shouted words, we slammed a door,
then loved each other even more.
Forgiveness spoke, in tone and touch,
a silent language saying much.

And though the years will stretch and bend,
this tether never finds an end.
For all they are, and all they'll be,
the best of them still lives in me.

PART III – THE FRACTURE

The Weight of Doing All

I wake before the morning light.
The house still echoes from the night.
The dishes wait. The floors complain,
a thousand tasks that call my name.

He says he'll help, just not today.
He's tired. He's worked. He's earned his stay.
But later never seems to come,
and all the noise turns my voice numb.

The kids demand; their breakfast's late.
I move through moments, worn by fate.
A spill to wipe, a shoe to tie,
a half-formed thought that drifts and dies.

He passes by, his coffee poured,
his smile a gift I can't afford.
He says, "You're better at these things,"
and leaves me with the day it brings.

By noon, I've lost what meals I've had.
By dusk, I lose what made me glad.
The kids are fed. The floor is swept.
The shadow I am still hasn't slept.

He calls it help to watch his own.
I call it grace to be alone.
A shower's peace, a stolen sigh,
a moment's breath before goodbye.

I love them, God. I love them still.
But love alone won't fill this will.
Each day I fade, ever small,
beneath the weight of doing all.

The Vampire

He slumps into the waiting chair,
the room grows still, the heavy air.
"I'm such a mess," he breathes, contrite,
"I never do a damn thing right."

She kneels beside him, meek, aware,
her voice a bandage placed with care.
"Here, love," she murmurs, "take what's mine.
My strength, my ground, my only spine."

He sighs and leans, begins to feed,
his grief a mouth, his want a need.
She pours herself a constant stream
to keep afloat his wavering dream.

But warmth in him won't linger long;
the need returns, the pull is strong.
She's not yet healed, not yet refilled,
still he drinks deep; her will lies killed.

She smiles, though hollow, dry, and thin,
a pale remnant of who she'd been.
He sleeps restored, she cannot rest,
the life-force drains within her chest.

The Turning

I tell him how his words last night
still echo sharp and don't feel right.
He sighs and asks, "You think I meant
to make you feel a punishment?"

I start to cry, but now he's sore.
He says, "I can't do this anymore."
And somehow I'm the one he names,
the one who always takes the blame.

So I dry his tears, forget my own,
and hide the parts I've never shown.
He sleeps; I stare at ceiling beams.
My hurt goes missing while he dreams.

Shrinking

I learned to take up smaller space,
to fold my words, to stay in place,
to cross my legs, to mind my tone,
and never call a thing my own.

At work I shrink so they can speak.
Their voice is strong while mine grows weak.
I watch my credit slip from view.
The praise I earned bestowed anew.

At home, I hide the torch I bear,
so he can lead and not compare.
I hand him goals I've yet to chase,
then smile and call it love's embrace.

I paint my joy in muted hue,
so no one else feels less than true.
I starve my worth to keep them fed,
and learn to live where hope is shed.

They say I'm patient, mild, and sweet,
a masterpiece of self-deceit.
For every *yes*, a piece is gone.
For every piece, I break at dawn.

And bit by bit, I lose my mind
to fit the mold of humankind.
'Til nothing's left but what they need,
a bottled soul they barely heed.

The morning comes, I search the glass,
but find no figure looking back—
no body there, just void, no skin,
an echo slipping deep within.

The world goes on, its muted thrum,
while I dissolve, unseen, undone.
No scream, no sound, no trace, no pain,
just letting go of what remains.

The Colors I Erased

He loved my hair when it was long,
so I ignored what felt all wrong.
He said that curls weren't really me,
so straightened strands was what they'd be.

Tops too revealing, skirts too bold,
so I wore subtle, plain, controlled.
The lipstick shades he couldn't stand
were wiped away by my own hand.

He liked me lighter, liked me thin,
so I carved smaller into skin.
I counted bites, ignored the hunger,
believed the change was mine to conquer.

A chameleon in shifting tones,
I blended with the world he owned.
I wore the colors he allowed,
a life confined to keep him proud.

I trimmed myself to fit his dream,
a version built for his esteem.
Until the woman left behind
was one he made and none of mine.

The Storm Within Walls

He sighs, the sink chock-full of plates,
"You do it best, I'll just wait."
He smiles as if his praise were loving;
I clean, but in my head I'm cussing.

The trash, the bills, the daily din,
"You're just more patient," he says, then grins.
His comfort rests on what I give,
and I forget, it's *my* life to live.

The next fight starts with something small,
a word misplaced, a name recalled.
"You're wrong," he says, "you're mixing things,"
and doubt begins to pull at strings.

My memory tilts beneath his look,
and my reality has been shook.
He laughs, "You're overthinking it,"
my truth reduced until it fits.

I've stinging eyes, he pulls me near,
his cadence velvet, voice sincere.
"You know I didn't mean those words,
It's just been hard," his peace preferred.

And with my ribs tense from duress,
I hold his wounds, ignore my stress.
He cannot stand his face in glass,
the shame too sharp, the blame amassed.

So all his weight he lays on me,
his guilt renamed as honesty.
He wears denial like a shield,
and calls me cruel for what I've revealed.

The squall returns, the levee breaks,
I shout my grief, all his mistakes.
He stays unmoved, composed, apart,
while fury grips my unmoored heart.

He points and hisses, "Now look at you,"
his even words cut anger through.
The walls bear witness to it all,
he starts the fire, then blames the fall.

Just Sinking

She moves through days like sinking sand,
each step a drag she hadn't planned.
The world around her glides with ease,
on steady paths, with fluent breeze.

Her mind becomes a tightening snare,
each thought a struggle for fresh air.
She feels the pull beneath her feet,
a slow descent she can't defeat.

A web she never chose to weave
holds tight to every fear she grieves.
It clings to all she tries to do,
the simple tasks she once walked through.

They rise, they shine, they move, they glow;
she watches from the undertow.
And every time she tries to rise,
the sand climbs higher up her thighs.

She worries that she can't be sure
of what is real, of what is pure.
Gaslit echoes twist her view,
and make her question what is true.

No lifeline pulls her back to shore,
just sinking where she stood before.

PART IV – THE UNDOING

The Life That Stays Behind

The days grow thin, the hours drag,
the world keeps spinning though I still lag.
The air collects my swallowed words,
the *why* that trembles is unheard.

I tidy, scrub, meet all their needs,
a gardener sinking in the weeds.
I once was strength, and hope, and drive,
but now I struggle to survive.

Guilt creeps in, her cadence clear,
her muttered judgments pressing near,
You know that love should be all you need,
your wanting more is simply greed.

And so I stay along this road,
a toll that's due for what I owed.
Their laughter lifts the atmosphere,
but doesn't reach what's dying here.

The woman I was, fierce in her stride,
still fights for air under my hide.
I yearn for trails I once could roam,
the life I lived before this home.

Yet every time I seek escape,
my duties 'round my shoulders drape.
A roof over their heads, not mine,
a world that's built on my decline.

So I hang my spirit out to dry,
and hope that they don't see me cry.
And when the silence gathers deep,
I mourn the woman I could not keep.

Fault Line

I've braced through gales for far too long,
called splitting *stoic;* it was wrong.
Each urge to crumble went unspoken,
another vow to self I'd broken.

I built them up with careful plans
and spurned myself to meet demands.
Their tempers sparked, I took the fault,
and forced my anger to a halt.

Its crumbs ground down into the floor,
toothpaste splattered on the door.
A toilet seat I've wiped again,
the same small cuts that never end.

And let me try to make a call,
they charge the room, they need it all.
The seconds they'd idled, wanting none,
erupt the moment I want one.

The cleats forgotten, books misplaced,
a hundred tasks I can't retrace.
Though it seems a trivial thing,
it's where the hidden pressures cling.

For rage is born from love's neglect,
from being drained of self-respect,
from years of bracing to sustain
the pressure mounting in my brain.

And then it comes, no tempered quake,
but every fault inside me shakes.
A slam, a scream, a ruptured word,
a mother's voice, too harsh, was heard.

It's fire I never meant to throw,
a blast my children shouldn't know,
their startled eyes, how my words land,
the aftermath I hadn't planned.

The guilt hits hard, a choking wave,
I'd trade my soul for what I gave.
The silence after, sharp, obscene,
the wreckage where my love has been.

They say it's anger, sharp, unkind,
but it's the breaking of my mind.
It's grief that's worn her mother's skin,
the scream she stifled to love her kin.

And when it bursts, the ground will quake,
a fault line carved by what I take.
I'll clean again, I'll make it right,
then cry alone in restless night.

Tomorrow brings the worn routine,
the same face hiding what has been.
I'll brace the weight and smile, it seems,
a mother cracking at the seams.

Suspended

The mountains split, the roar was done,
the heat was heavy beneath the sun.
The planet hissed, the earth now steamed,
a fevered hush where fire had screamed.

No cry remained, no beating sound,
just smoke that hovered near the ground.
The sky held ash over earthen grill,
as if the world had lost its will.

No one runs, no voices call,
just echoes lingering from the fall.
Between the crack and what will come,
the heart waits molten, deaf and dumb.

After The Burning

The house is quiet, the anger gone,
its heat dissolving with the dawn.
The air saves outlines of the fight,
like smoke that stays long after night.

The rooms remember what I've said,
each syllable, a scar turned red.
The void clings tight, it feels alive,
a breath that asks how hope survives.

They sleep upstairs, their lashes wet,
and I replay what I regret.
The way their bodies flinched from mine,
as if my reach could cross a line.

I touch the doorframe, draw in the air,
and wish the hurt could vanish there.
If love were stronger, calm, and wise,
why can't it hide the fire inside?

I murmur scored apologies
to shadows kept in memories.
I smooth their blankets, brush their hair,
a prayer disguised as mother's care.

The rage is gone, but in its place,
a hollow ache, a vacant space.
In that void, I see the cost,
the tender parts of me I've lost.

Still in the pitch, they come to light,
and mercy meets me in their sight.
For even ash can hold a spark,
and love returns within the dark.

The Stranger in the House

We drift like strangers through every room,
the air is stale, perfumed with gloom.
Your movement passes, known too well,
you are the man I cannot quell.

The plates still clink, the floorboards groan,
each sound a story all its own.
We talk of bills, of school, of rain,
just words to dull what now remains.

At night we lie there, side by side,
two continents the years divide.
No warmth to bridge, no touch to find,
the sheets divide what once aligned.

The children laugh, their brightness shows,
they never see what distance knows.
We smile for them, perform our parts,
a home of walls but not of hearts.

I yearn for when your words felt safe,
for memories of your sweet embrace.
Now love's a door I can't get through,
it reaches still, but not for you.

The House That Words Undid

The vows once murmured soft as rain
now crack like stones cast hard with blame.
The halls recall our wedding song,
but every note now feels so wrong.

Your voice once silk that eased my fears,
now cuts through stillness, sharp as shears.
The tongue that sweetened every night
has learned to twist, to scorch, to bite.

The hands that mapped me warm and slow,
now fists of anger he may throw.
The arms that once were safe, contained,
stand crossed, accusing, cold, restrained.

The light that bathed our morning bed
now flickers harsh, then turns to red.
The life we shared now stands undone,
two halves cut clean, no longer one.

And still I stand within these beams,
although a blade splits through the seams.
To hold what's gone, to grieve what stayed,
the house we built, the one we splayed.

The Weary One

She's weary of mending, of lifting, of strain,
of holding the world while she steadily drains.
She listens for solace, where the willows all weep,
where mists drift like secrets the night longs to keep.

She doesn't need fixing, doesn't need praise,
she just needs the mercy of much kinder days.
Let her lay down her head where the dusk starts to creep,
let her drift into calm, let her finally sleep.

For she's shaped her whole life from the throb in her chest,
now she's learning that grace can teach her to rest.
And somewhere beyond all the noise and the strain,
the forest calls to her—she's home once again.

For My Sister

For weeks I walked and did not know
the life I carried ebbed in stow.
A cradle turned to something cold,
a story ended, never told.

They spoke of nature, cruel and all,
as if that knowledge would halt my fall,
as if it touched the wounds I brave
from being both your home and grave.

A plush gray elephant that smelled brand new,
a gift for hands that never grew.
It waits upon a quiet shelf,
a memory I keep for myself.

My body meant to guard and give,
had kept you long past when you lived.
A vessel never meant for death,
yet holding what had lost its breath.

Beneath the lights they took you then,
piece after piece, again and again.
Your only birth, a silent part,
no head to crown, no cry to start.

No answers came for what went wrong,
No gender given to belong.
A child unseen, a truth not kept,
A nameless sorrow where you slept.

Some wounds don't heal; they only stay,
agony carried day by day.
A lullaby I never sang,
your future gone before it rang.

Vanishing

I wanted to vanish, not die, not decay,
just melt into mist and be carried away,
to drift through the trees where nature can speak,
where time moves in twilight with no more to seek.

To be fog on the water, the air through the pine,
a ripple that murmurs, *this moment is mine.*
No names, no demands, no past to forgive,
just learning how quiet can teach me to live.

And the forest replied, *you're not meant to flee,*
you can fade for a while and still choose to be.
Rest here for a while where no one can see,
and find the belonging that waits within me.

Grace

I used to hold you in my blame.
Your negligence wore my childhood's name.
The burden you dropped became my own,
a trauma I outgrew alone.

But now I see how hearts can break,
how hope bends thin for living's sake,
how love can bow beneath the weight,
and tenderness steals into slate.

You never asked, nor made amends,
but time grew soft where fury ends.
I see the phantoms that you chased,
and grant you grace time can't erase.

For though you failed to hear my voice,
I know you felt you had no choice,
and in that drought I learned to be
a mother still with empathy.

The Hidden Place Within Me

I used to dance inside my skin,
a feral spirit I had been,
but time's devotion leaked like a sieve
and rewrote the way I had to live.

Mother, wife, such holy names,
yet underneath, they cloud the frames.
I pour, I serve, I spend, I lend,
and lose myself to them again.

Each morning starts with someone's need,
each night I wilt from all I bleed.
I feed my kin from my own bone,
then wonder why I feel alone.

They call it joy, this sacred art,
but even joy can fracture heart.
For every smile I've stitched in place,
I've hidden tears I can't erase.

And under all the noise and years,
beneath the guilt, the weight, the fears,
there stirs a song, a low refrain,
a siren beckoning my name.

She's found where shifting branches fall,
where she can rise and stand up tall.
Within a cabin inside my mind,
a refuge life won't let me find.

She's not a mother, not a wife,
she's just the soul that forged this life.
She's carried on the cedar's breeze,
she glides like sunlight through the leaves.

Her soul is mine, her spirit free,
she is the truest form of me.
Her desires form with ardent grace,
and I return to that hidden place.

And when the world pulls me apart,
I'll close my eyes and find her spark.
For though I stagger, wear, and spin,
the woman I was still lives within.

So let them take, I will remain,
through love, loss, joy, and pain.
For deep beneath what they all see,
there waits the one who's truly me.

The Evidence

A text you hid but didn't clear,
a name you shouldn't keep so near.
A bra that wasn't bought by me,
left hidden in the laundry sea.

A night outstretched, too long, too late,
your half-truths failed to replicate.
I traced the shape of your deceit,
one clue, then two beneath my feet.

My stomach dropped, my breath held fast,
a rising choke I couldn't pass.
Not grief, not rage, but something raw,
the first cold twist of what I saw.

No shouting yet, no fractures loud,
just quiet proof, a creeping shroud.
Betrayal has come without a sound,
my breaking point is now unbound.

The Breaking Point

The house ignites with violent sound,
each word a weapon, swung unbound.
You curse, I scream, the walls recoil,
our love reduced to ash and soil.

Your eyes are fire, mine strike back,
two storms collide and split the cracks.
The plates explode, the curtains tear,
God help the ghosts still trapped in there.

Just Today

She stays out late. He's not at home.
She's at the bar. She drinks alone.
She finds her comfort in the bottle,
no holding back, she goes full throttle.

She tilts her head back, lets her mind deaden,
as wolves prepare for Armageddon.
Vultures gather to feast upon
the carcass of her vows long gone.

At first it's glances from across the room,
still as nightfall, dark as gloom.
Falcon eyes that sweep and scan,
searching for the break in man.

The grief that clings to her like smoke,
a signal rising to provoke.
It marks her steps with something frail,
a scent for them to stalk her trail.

She paces toward the bathroom's haze,
a corridor of watchful gaze.
A shadow slips to block her pace,
its presence pressing into place.

Hot, stinking breath invades her air,
a sour warmth she cannot bear.
And venom drips in words obscene,
a serpent's whisper, low and keen.

His hand is bold, his grin too near,
a trespass steeped in thick stale beer.
She twists away, her pulse a drum,
her mind gone silent, body numb.

The door ahead becomes her prayer.
She breaks his grasp and stumbles there.
She locks the stall, hands on the wall,
steadying breath so she won't fall.

She's panting now, her body shakes.
Her skin remembers every stake.
She's safe, for now. She knows the play.
She escaped this time, but *just today*.

The Leaving

He hurls a lamp; it bursts in light,
his sharp teeth gnash as fear takes flight.
She moves through chaos, calm and slow,
her voice a firm, unyielding *no*.

She packs her life with practiced grace,
the fury swirling 'round her space.
Glass shatters close; she does not turn,
she's walked through worse; let cities burn.

The screen door moans; the morning glows,
her poise is louder than his throws.
The car hums low; her path is clear.
She leaves and never checks the mirror.

The Empty House

The walls exhale, the echoes fade,
no laughter left, no plans we made.
The air still keeps what once was said,
but even ghosts have gone to bed.

The floors don't creak, the light stands still,
the rooms no longer bend our will.
What once was war is now release.
An empty house at last, at peace.

Life Sentence

I pictured years that felt like light,
a shared horizon, clear and bright.
A house that held our hopes in place,
your hand in mine, a smoother pace.

But slowly love became a chain,
a private grief, a daily drain.
The ring I wore, no symbol then,
just metal locking me again.

A finger cuff, a tethered hold,
a story tightening as it unfolds.
Each vow that should have set me free
became the shackles anchoring me.

And when I left, I thought I'd break
the pull of him with one clean shake.
I signed the lines they said were mine,
but signatures don't sever time.

For he still reaches through our kids,
demands, critiques, rewrites, forbids.
Control reborn in stricter ways,
a pressure threaded through my days.

Some sentences don't end with tears,
they stretch across the coming years,
disguised as parenting, thinly veiled.
Another way I'm watched, derailed.

I broke the marriage, cut the ties,
yet still his will is in my life.
This freedom's thin, and truth is clear:
I left, but he is always here.

PART V – THE RISING

She Keeps Rising

She's walked through wreckage of another kind,
its muted chapters have seared her mind.
She's bit her tongue for far too long,
the tension snapped against the wrong.

She's mourned a love that slipped from sight,
She's watched her trust drain out by spite,
She's learned devotion's heavy toll
when no one stayed to hold her soul.

Yet she stands, bare feet unbowed,
beneath the mass the years allowed.
Her tongue, once trembling, now stakes claim,
her scars remembered, but not her shame.

She learned herself through darker hours,
not in delight, but fallen towers.
For every wound that split her skin
revealed a force once locked within.

And though the world may never know
the war she wages all alone,
she gathers nerve from ruin's crown.
A woman lost, a woman found.

Clarity

Lightning flashed across her mind,
revealing patterns she could find.
A safety net she had called home,
a web revealed, once cloaked by gloam.

And seeing clear what shaped her then,
she chose what won't shape her again.
At last she sees what held her fast
and frees the child from her past.

Where Quiet Lives

She lingers where the dawn breaks through,
where skies awaken, washed in blue.
Her steps unhurried, steady, free,
the world leans in to let her be.

She speaks in slow, unrushed tones
to ancient trees and weathered stones.
They hold her thoughts, they draw her near,
their leaves translate what souls can't hear.

She sips on solace through simple days,
finds beauty cloaked in common ways.
A kettle's whirl, a window's glint,
the due return of her footprint.

She learned tranquility is not a post,
but found when repose becomes her host.
And when the noise slips through the cracks,
she savors sands within the glass.

For in the lull the world forgives,
and she remembers
where quiet lives.

The Bloom After

She shed the weight the years had grown,
the dronings that were not her own.
The mirrors cracked, the masks unmade,
and in their shards the truth displayed.

The girl who bent so others thrived,
who dimmed herself to stay alive,
now blooms from ashes fierce and brave,
a garden rising from her grave.

She does not heed the world's command;
it comes to her, it takes her hand.
She walks where sorrow once had fed,
The past no longer paints her red.

Forgiveness winds in tender vine,
and all her losses now align.
Each scattered piece she could not save,
now forms the path she dares to brave.

For every break that split her heart,
became the space where love could start.
The kind she'd never known before,
for her, the one worth fighting for.

She learned her worth was hers to seize,
not earned through yielding just to please.
Now courage moves through her, it's clear,
the rise of woman without fear.

She's not the woman she once planned,
but one the universe had spanned.
And every scar, each shattered part,
redrew the path back to her heart.

Caring Too Much

I cared till my spirit forgot how to rest,
till love became labor that hollowed my chest.
I harbored the rapids till my banks washed away,
till a stone in the shallows urged, *you cannot stay.*

*The breeze on the water said, you cannot save
each leaf from the current, each heart from the wave.
But you can step out where the swift river slows,
and loosen the burdens that you never chose.
For love isn't drowning to show you can swim,
it's knowing when edges turn ragged and thin.*

So I step from the waters, reclaim my own spark,
keep only the pieces that brighten the dark.

Becoming Whole

She wakes unhurried with the dawn,
the bulk she bore at last is gone.
No roles imposed, no part to play,
just open sky to mold her way.

She treads the astral realms with poise,
high above the crowd's harsh noise.
Her life no longer up for trade,
no shallow love can make her fade.

She tends her light like seeded stars,
with quiet sight that mends her scars.
She shapes new worlds from broken past,
her orbit widening, true and vast.

Supernovas create their blasts,
yet she just blinks and moves right past.
She knows now when to speak, to rest,
to love herself and choose what's best.

Her bliss, it shows, no veil, no guise,
the stars reflected in her eyes.
For all she's lost, she's gained the whole.
The cosmos thrive inside her soul.

I Let My Curls Be Free

No scent of scorched or smoking hair,
no iron hiss, no heated glare,
no more searing of my skin,
to press what's wild and lock it in.

I cup each curl, damp and unstyled,
and find the cheer I lost as child.
They spring and fall, they twist, they play.
I wouldn't trade their willful sway.

The world still praised the polished few,
but I saw beauty breaking through.
Each coil a story, fierce unknown,
a path my younger self disowned.

Now rain can fall, I do not hide,
each drop a blessing, sanctified.
I walk unbrushed for all I've cried,
now curls and self the same inside.

A World Without Masks

I grew up in a world askew,
where lies were stitched in every view,
where truth cut deep, so people hid,
and wrapped themselves in comfort's bid.

But I was born with sight innate,
to see the worlds that others hate.
I question every thought I trace,
each whisper moving through my space.

I tear apart the things I say,
to see what truth might slip away.
I hold my flaws beneath the flame.
I never flinch or shift the blame.

They call it harsh, this way I see,
but all I want is honesty.
No pretty masks, no softened tone,
just truth that meets me, fully known.

This gift, this curse, its edges sting,
to see what's false in everything.
To guard what's real, though most deceive,
stay rooted while they make believe.

But I'm unmoved, though hope feels thin,
I'll wear no mask upon my skin.
For though this world may warp and sway,
my compass leads me all the way.

So let them warp, let others sway,
I'll meet the dark, clear as day.
For honesty is not unkind,
It's just the way I stay aligned.

I'll walk through twilight, gloom, and bane,
wash off the falsehoods in the rain.
And though the crowd cannot conceive,
I'll stay the course and never leave.

What I Keep

I said yes when I meant decline,
believing virtue must align.
But every nod became a chain
that bound my worth to others' gain.

I learned to yield to guard the peace,
to trade what's mine for their release,
but the blood was boiling in my veins,
as conviction pulled at the reins.

At first each *no* felt sharp, extreme,
too loud, too much, too far, obscene.
But what felt harsh was simply fair,
my stance reclaiming I'd been there.

They said I'd changed, grown cold, unkind,
but I was just reclaiming spine.
I learned that peace is not submission,
and love need not mean self-omission.

Each *no* I speak unbinds the chains,
each line I draw restores my name.
To guard myself is not betrayal;
it shields my heart when vows may fail.

The key was mine; it always fit.
I'd held it blind in my own fist.
The lock released without a sound,
and all I'd lost had now been found.

The Wholeness of Me

I do not wait for someone's thrill.
I'm whole in this, though wanting still.
To want and never ache or cling,
that is the purest kind of thing.

PART VI – THE TABLE
(THE RETURN)

The Breath

The path is cotton under tread,
The morning lifts its golden head.
Each breath a mist, the cold made clear.
It fills my chest and draws me near.

The mountains gleam with crowns of snow,
the rain-wet ground fragrant below.
A zephyr drifts through the glade
and settles thoughts as burdens fade.

I exhale slow and feel strain cease,
as life renews in small degrees.
For once, the air belongs to me,
and breathing is enough to be.

The Measure of Love

He reached for me; I did not run,
nor let his touch imply I'd won.
I once mistook a grasp for grace,
a claim for love, a cage for place.

I've known the masks that danger wears,
the charm he hides, the words he snares,
the tricks he used to cut a deal,
the harm he caused, that he said *heals*.

Yet I still search for what is real,
a compassion no fear can steal.
So I let kindness linger near,
and trust seeps in, though slow, sincere.

If love persists when not pursued,
nor bargained, bought, or harshly wooed,
then maybe this is true love's key,
to be with him and still have me.

And So I Stayed

I did not know that love could stay,
not burn or break or drift away.
I thought it always came with cost,
a piece of self that must be lost.

He came with hands that didn't take,
an open heart, not one to fake.
He listened first and met my gaze,
a comfort longed for all my days.

He speaks and all the noise runs still,
no warping truth, no hardened will.
His love does not demand or test;
it builds a home inside my chest.

No edge, no storm, no waiting dread,
no careful steps, no words unsaid,
Just loyalty that doesn't wane,
A hand that never brings me pain.

His arms encircle me, not tight,
no need to brace, no urge for flight.
I melt instead, let armor yield,
as I take in what trust revealed.

No need to earn, no price to pay,
just being present day after day.
I never knew that love could be
so full, so sure, so safe, so free.

He never asked that I shrink small,
nor lift the load to prove it all.
He built a life beside, not through,
and taught me love could still be true.

My children's laughter fills the air.
He kneels to meet them; he is there.
He teaches strength, not shame or fear.
His presence makes the whole world clear.

And I, once fractured, whittled, worn,
have found a place I thought was torn.
No crown, no rescue, no crusade,
just love that heals.
And so I stayed.

For the Mother Who Hopes After Loss

When two faint lines began to rise,
my heartbeat stumbled, quick, surprised.
Joy flickered first, then fear struck fast,
a gloom was lurking from the past.

I held my breath through every week,
each flutter small, each symptom meek.
I counted days as if they'd end,
the weight of grief I couldn't fend.

I dreamed in color, prayed in gray,
unsure which truth would win the day.
Hope pressed against the walls of doubt,
a trembling glow still holding out.

I guarded you with watchful thoughts,
my voice was choked, my prayers were fraught.
Each doctor's room became a test,
I braced for loss, I begged for rest.

But still you grew, a steady spark,
a lantern rising through the dark.
Your heart had drummed a trembling beat,
a promise forming, small, complete.

And when the night at last arrived,
when pain announced you'd soon survive,
I held the breath that grief had taught,
then let it go, each fear I'd fought.

You broke into the world with cries
that rinsed the sorrow from my eyes.
Warm skin on mine, a living truth,
the balm that stitched the seam of youth.

I loved you with inspired awe,
while harboring ruin, feeling raw.
But from the ache of what I'd lost,
I found a strength that knew the cost.

And though one child I'll never hold
still lives inside the grief I fold,
your light does not replace that name.
It grows beside it all the same.

You are the color after rain,
the slow undoing of my pain.
A dawn impossible to keep,
and mine to cradle, awake, not sleep.

Bring Yourself to the Table

She built her life from weary bone,
A table carved from self alone.
Her back the wood, her hands the frame,
her love the labor none could name.

They gathered close, her joy, her kin,
their laughter soft against her skin.
They broke their bread, their food dished out.
They feasted long while she missed out.

Beneath their glee she hid her cries,
as agony pooled behind her eyes.
While crumbs fell down to where she kneeled,
she ate the scraps their love revealed.

Each morsel small, a fleeting grace,
enough to keep her in her place.
She whispered prayers the floor could hear,
for someone's heart to draw her near.

The tile felt cold, her body weak,
her mouth too tired to let her speak.
Yet still she held through every year
the weight of love, the grip of fear.

But something stirred within her spine,
a tremor soft, a hard-drawn line.
She saw the crumbs, the empty floor,
and knew she'd bow her back no more.

With trembling hands she raised the wood,
and stood up as only mothers could.
The table shook, the feast was spilled,
a startled pause, the moment chilled.

Then gently she began to say,
"It's time we eat a different way.
I've carried long but now I find,
this feast was made with me in mind."

She propped the legs, she took her seat,
her heart now certain, her breath complete.
No longer bent, no longer small,
she smiled and said, "We'll share it all."

The children laughed, the love engraved,
serenity, once forgotten, saved.
No longer scaffold, nor the floor,
she brought the table and so much more.

The Cabin We Built

Once this cabin lived inside me,
a quiet place no one could find me.
Where calm returned, and stillness grew,
and I remembered what was true.

But love came knocking at my door.
Their laughter spilled across the floor.
I feared the noise, the mess, the strain.
Would peace withstand their joy again?

Yet here we are in fire's light,
our faces warmed, our hearts made right.
The forest hums, the oaks stand tall,
and relief moves through it all.

The streams out back once sang of gold,
of miners chasing wealth untold.
But I have found the richer vein,
the jewel of love that will remain.

No pick, no pan, no mountain claim,
just hands that build and hearts the same.
My treasure glints beneath the pine,
this love, this life, this gold is mine.

No taking now, no giving small,
we share the valley, wide it sprawls.
Moss blankets earth, in gentle spread,
a place where I can rest my head.

This cabin once was just escape,
now we have given it a shape.
Not built of wood, or walls confined,
but roots and laughter intertwined.

The Seat Beside Them

There's sunlight resting on the floor,
the kind I used to chase before.
The house exhales a quiet air,
contentment whispers everywhere.

No one's calling from the hall,
no rush to serve, no wait at all.
My love still gives, but so do they.
We meet in balance day by day.

The table's full, but I can sit,
I take my place, not under it.
My name is mine, well-lived, well-worn,
a quiet strength in me, reborn.

He looks at me and truly sees
the woman whole, the one who's free.
No warrant flashed, he takes my hand—
just adoration without demand.

I watch them grow, yet stay my own,
their joy the soil my roots have known.
No altar built, no prayer to say,
just cloudless skies to bless the day.

The ache is gone, the lesson stays:
to love myself in all the ways.
From the ash the phoenix soars,
a woman crowned by what she bore.

EPILOGUE

The Invitation

Come sit beside the tender flame.
No need for armor, fear, or shame.
The world is wide, but here's your space,
a softer home, a kind embrace.

You've walked through fire; now simply be.
You've reached the table.

You are free.

For the Woman Who Sat Quietly

For the woman who carried this book home, maybe tucked between errands, or found in a moment when she needed to feel less alone, this is for you.

For the one who has swallowed her voice to keep the peace, who has kept the house standing on her own tired shoulders, who has loved and lost and still chooses gentleness.

May these pages remind you: you were never meant to vanish inside your giving. Your softness is not a weakness, and your stillness is not your end. You are allowed to be both the flame and the calm that follows it.

You belong at the table too.

Even the ash became soil beneath her feet.

Acknowledgments

To my sons—
you were the anchor that held me in the storm
and the light that pulled me out.
Every step I took towards healing
was one I wanted you to witness.
Thank you for giving me a reason
to become the woman I needed to be
and for reminding me, every day,
that love can rebuild, what fear once broke.

To my mother—
even where the story hurt,
I see now the weight you carried.
Parts of you live in these pages,
and I return them to you with grace,
softened by time,
understood in ways I could not have seen as a child.

To my sisters—
for the childhood we survived,
for the strength we learned too young,
and for the bond that outlived everything that meant to break it—
you are woven into every line.

To Ethan—
thank you for the steadiness,
your patience,
and the kind of love that never asked me to vanish
so that you could shine.
You showed me that gentleness can be real,
that safety is possible,
and that a partner can stay without taking.

To the women who find themselves in these poems—
may these pages remind you of your worth,
your voice,
and the truth that you were never meant
to carry everything alone.
If any line here mirrors your story,
I hope it also reflects your strength.

About the Author

Kelly Marsh is a wife, mother, poet, and lifelong over-giver learning how to take her own seat at the table. For years she carried households, relationships, and expectations on her back, mistaking self-abandonment for love and endurance for worth. Therapy, hard conversations, and the slow work of setting boundaries began to teach her a different way.

This book was born from that process—written for women who have been the glue, the caregiver, the strong one, or the quiet one who keeps the peace at any cost. Her poems explore generational trauma, religious and cultural pressure, the weight of motherhood and marriage, and the long journey back to self, without losing the people we love.

Bring Yourself to the Table is not a manual or a set of instructions—it is a record of one woman learning, slowly and painfully, that it is both kind and necessary to have limits. But more than that, it is an invitation. The lessons within it are not hers alone; they are truths any woman can grow into. Through each piece, Kelly hopes readers will see themselves, recognize their worth, and feel empowered to take up their rightful space at the table of their own lives. She wants these pages to feel like a gentle companion in your own healing. A reminder that you are not too much, not asking for too much, and never meant to disappear inside your giving.

When she isn't writing, Kelly finds grounding in nature, introspection, and the simple joys of building a life shaped by both strength and softness. She believes deeply that women deserve rest, wholeness, and the freedom to be fully themselves—no shrinking, no silence, no apologies.

www.ingramcontent.com/pod-product-compliance
Lightning Source LLC
Chambersburg PA
CBHW020945090426
42736CB00010B/1275